Hetty's
thumb sucking habit

Barbara Bechtold-Dingemans

Written by:
Barbara Bechtold-Dingemans

Illustrated by:
Barbara Bechtold-Dingemans
and edited by Cody Verhagen

Translated from Dutch by:
Susanne Chumbley

Published by:
Graviant educational publications, Doetinchem, The Netherlands

© August 2016

This work is copyrighted.
All rights reserved by Graviant educational publications, Doetinchem, The Netherlands, telephone 0031314345400. No part of this publication may be reproduced, stored in a retrieval system or transmitted in any other form or by any other means, electronic, mechanical, photocopying, recording or otherwise without the prior written permission of the publisher.

ISBN 978-9491337888

Although this book is compiled with care, neither the authors nor the publisher accepts any liability for the fact that the use of what is offered does not meet the needs or expectations of the end user, nor for any errors or omissions.

Introduction

Through my work as a speech therapist, I meet a lot of children who, as a result of thumb sucking (or using a pacifier) have misaligned teeth or an incorrect way of swallowing or speaking (lisping). Thumb sucking and using a pacifier are referred to as 'dysfunctional orofacial habits'. To solve this problem the Oro- Myofunctional therapy (OMFT) has been developed and is used by speech therapists, in cooperation with dentists and orthodontists, to teach children how to eliminate these dysfunctional orofacial habits. With therapy, the misalignment of the teeth can often be reduced or even eliminated.

This book shows parents and children, in a clear but playful way, what happens when your child sucks their thumb. You also see what happens afterwards when your child stops sucking their thumb and what happens to the thumb, teeth and tongue. This book hasn't been made to shame your child for thumb-sucking, but to show why it would be better to give it up.

Hetty's thumb is often not happy because he is never free.
All the time he has to go in Hetty's mouth and that's not very healthy you see.

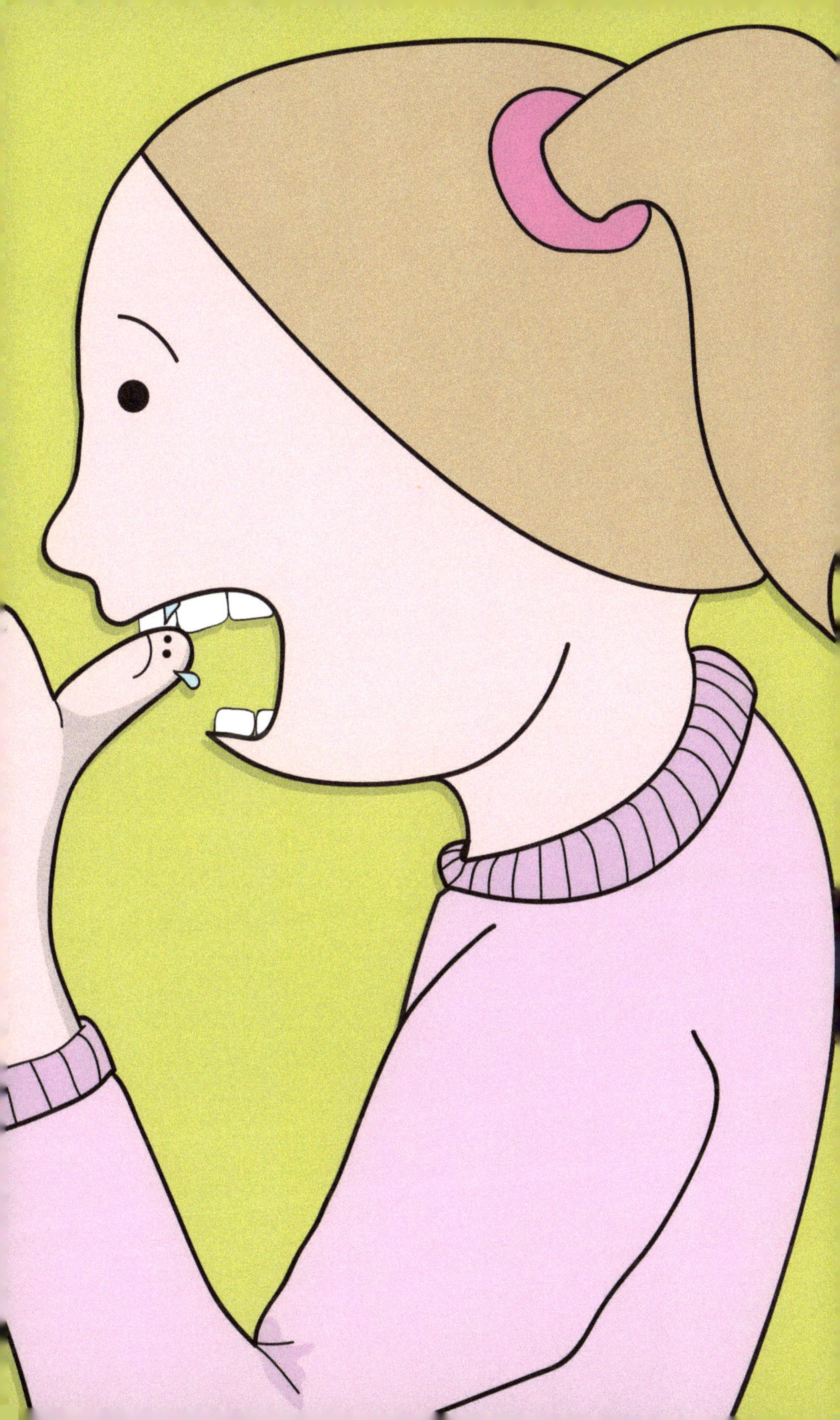

It is dark and wet
in Hetty's mouth
and her thumb has had
enough.
It is far too hot in there
he is really finding it
tough.

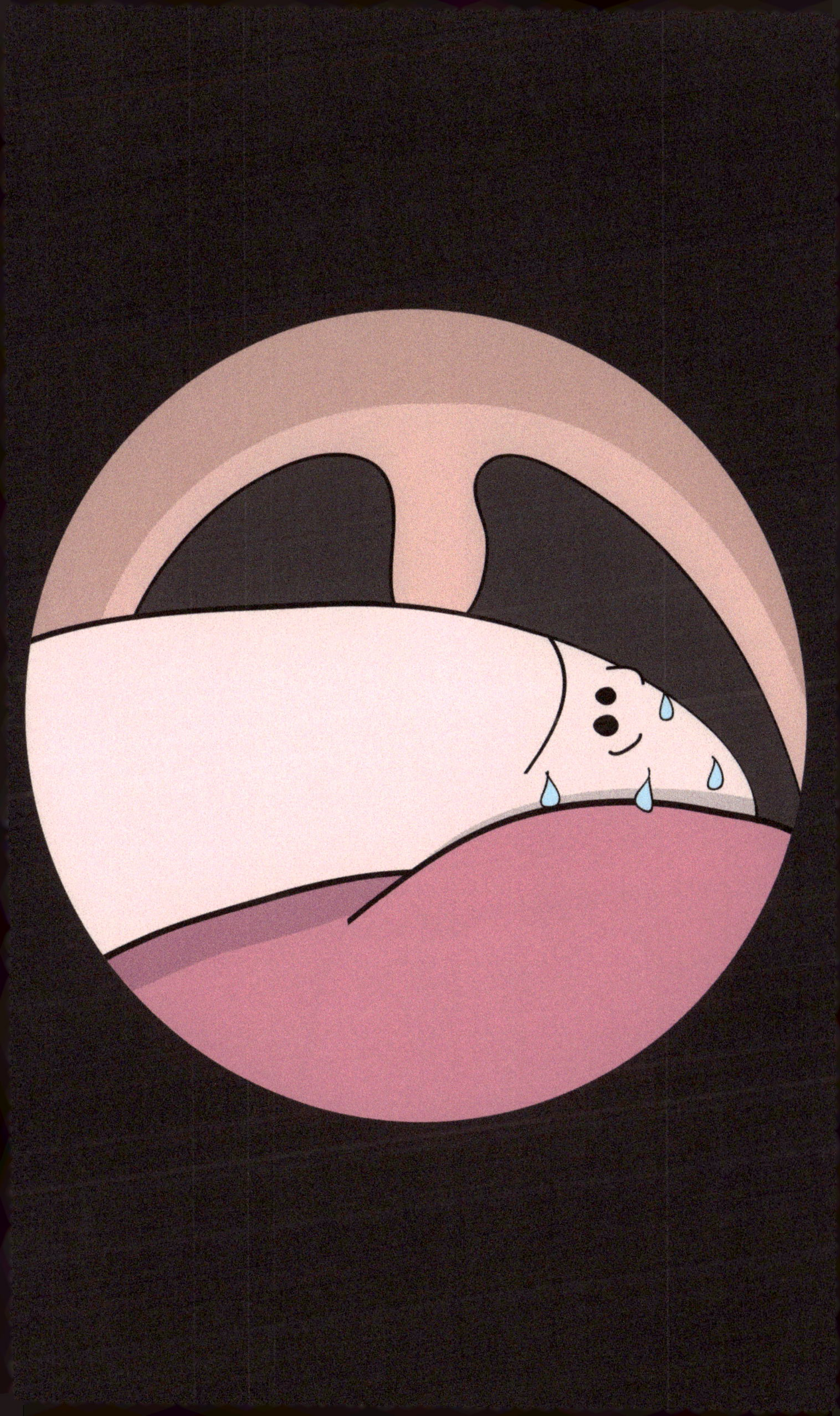

Hetty's teeth are
not happy either.
Look at them, sitting
in a row.
They don't want the thumb
pushing against them.
No, they rather see him go.

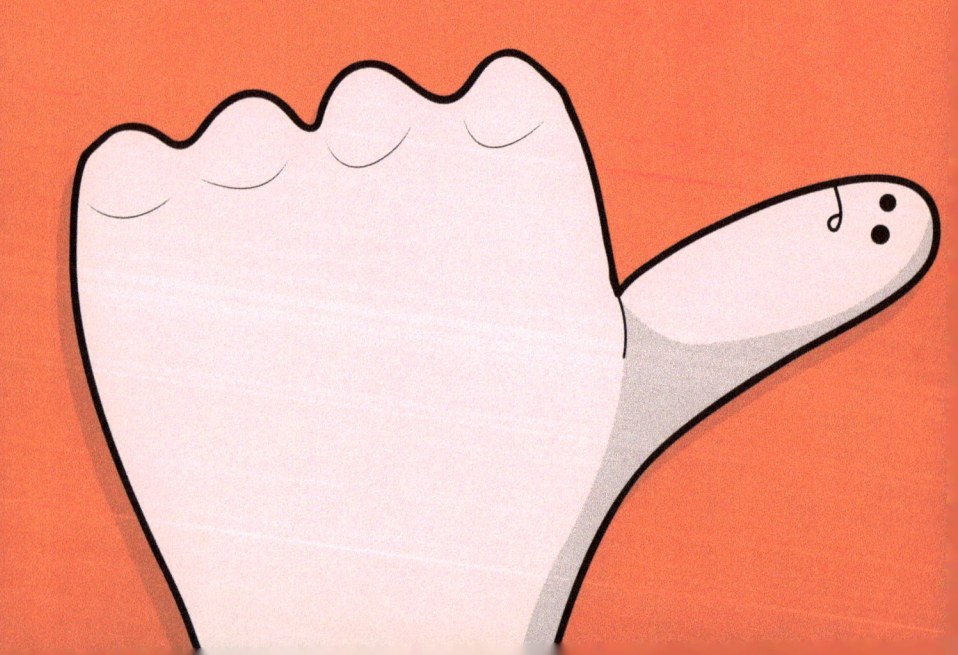

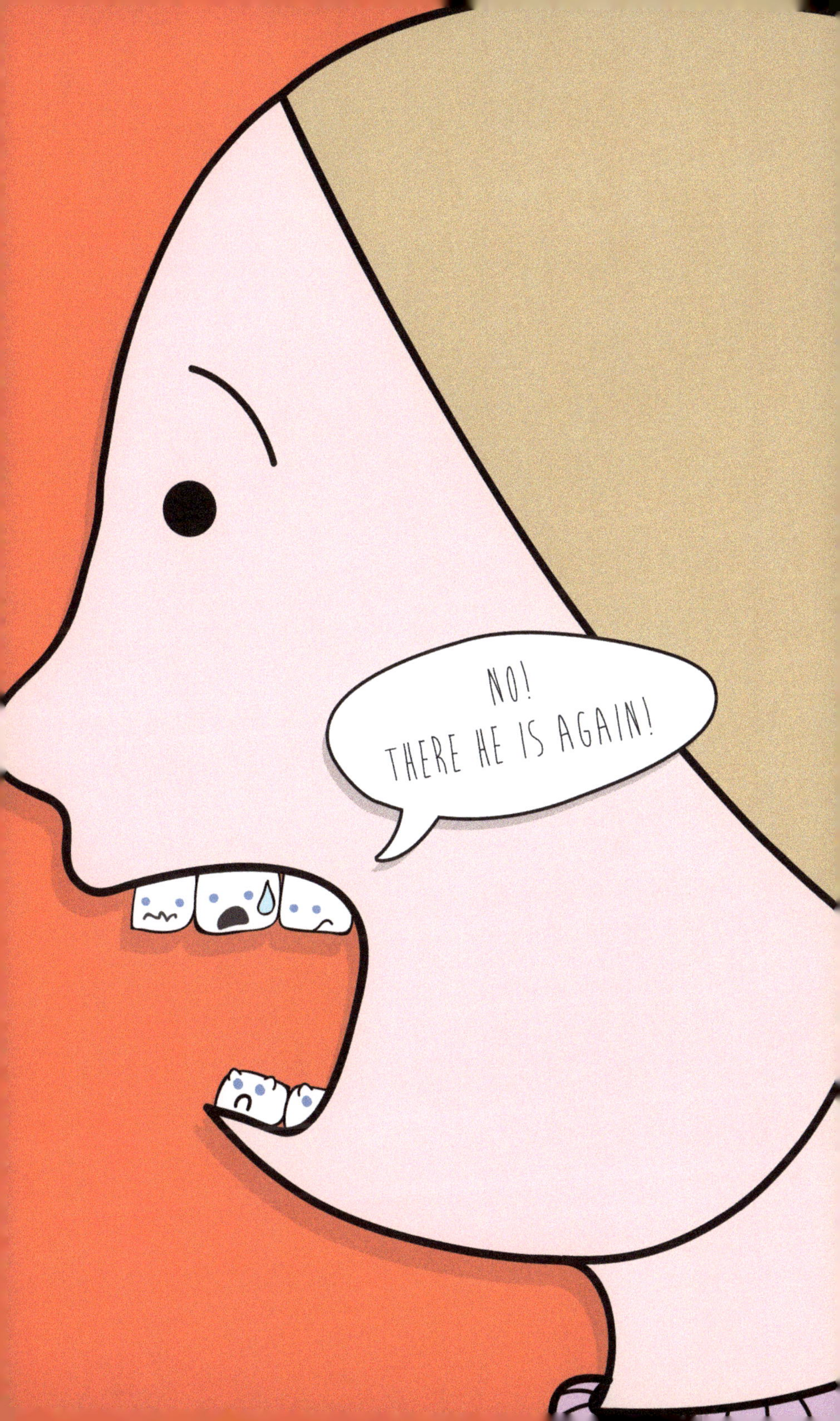
NO!
THERE HE IS AGAIN!

Maybe this sounds a bit strange but he pushes the teeth out of the way. The top teeth get pushed forward and that's not where they like to stay.

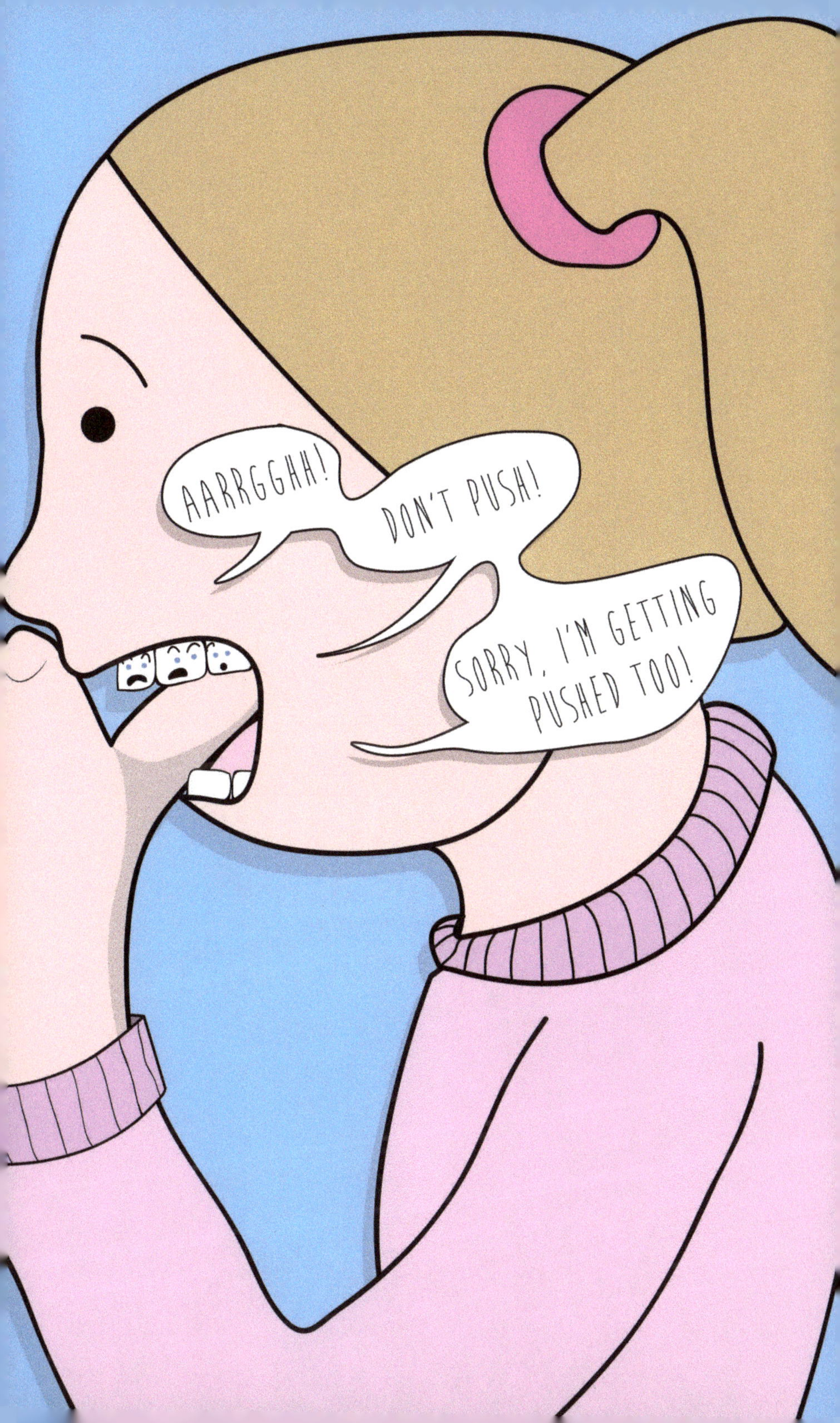
AARRGGHH!
DON'T PUSH!
SORRY, I'M GETTING PUSHED TOO!

The tongue is also
not very happy.
The thumb pushes him
all the way down.
"All the way to the bottom
of Hetty's mouth",
he says with a frown.

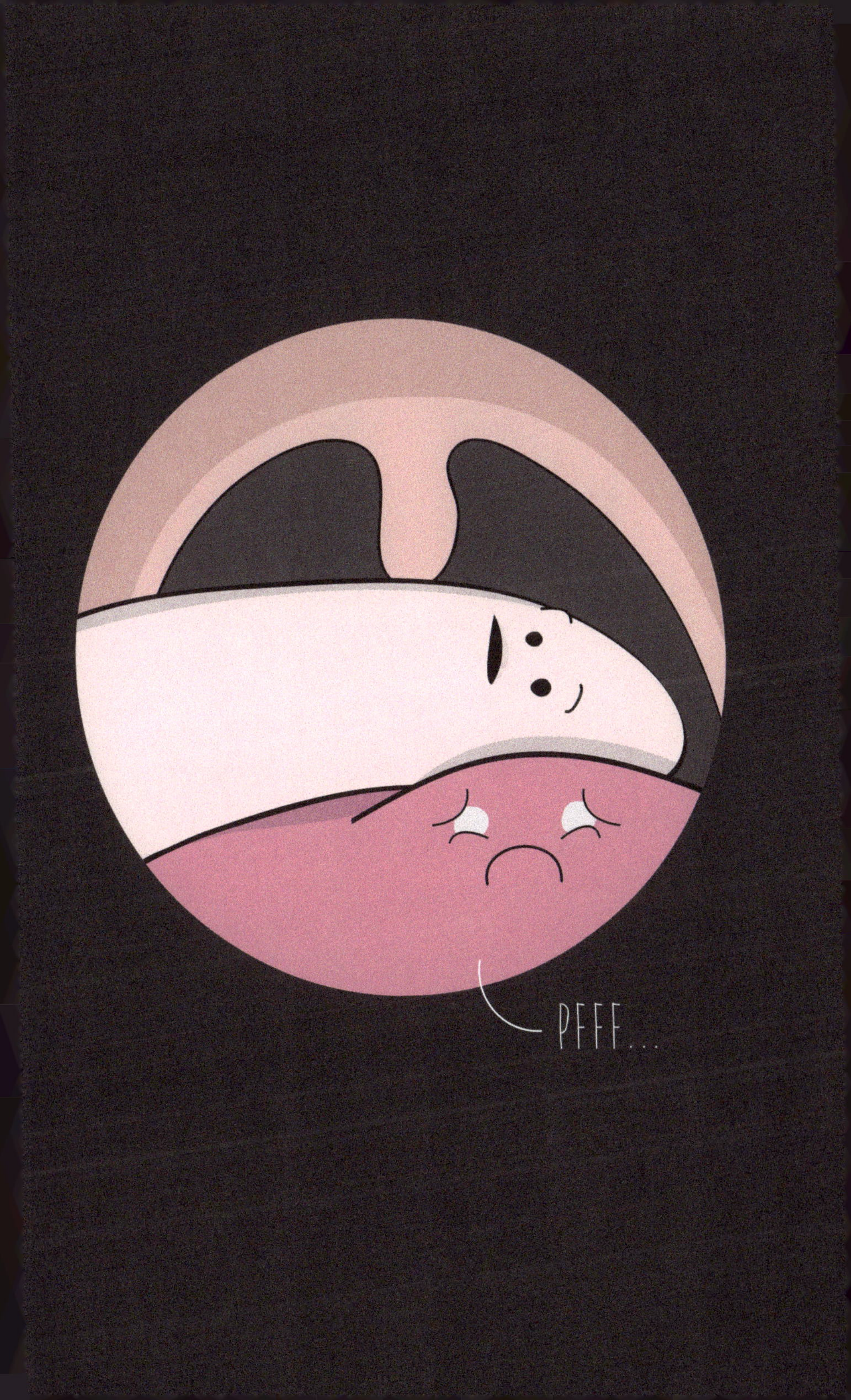
PFFF...

> HEY, TONGUE! ARE YOU COMING BACK UP?

This makes the tongue very lazy and gets him often in a bad mood.
He is getting weaker and weaker,
he doesn't work so hard,
he is one lazy dude.

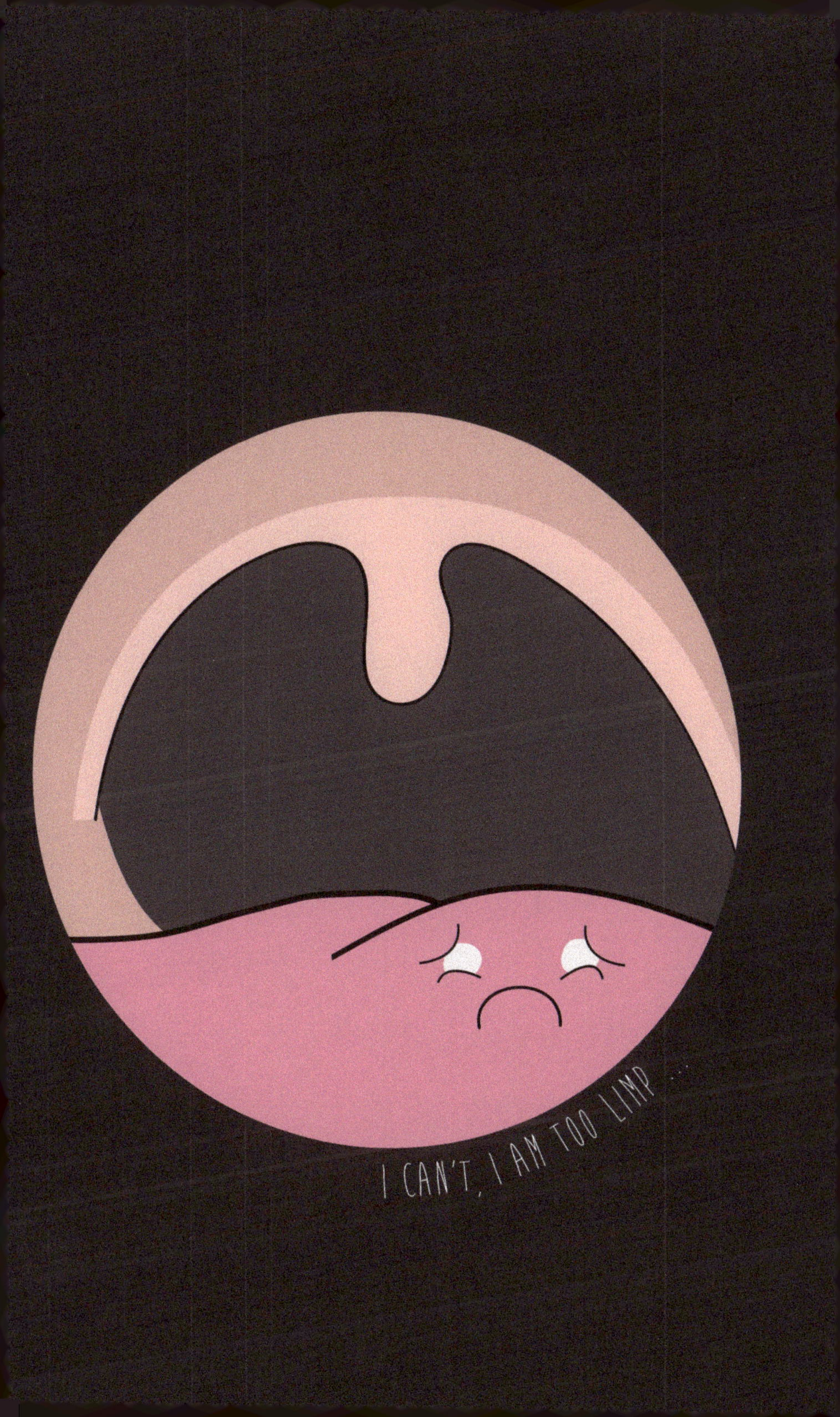
I CAN'T, I AM TOO LIMP ....

Hetty's teeth are nearly pushed all the way out. Her mum thinks it is unhealthy.

"That tongue is far too limp!" Shouts her dad out loud.

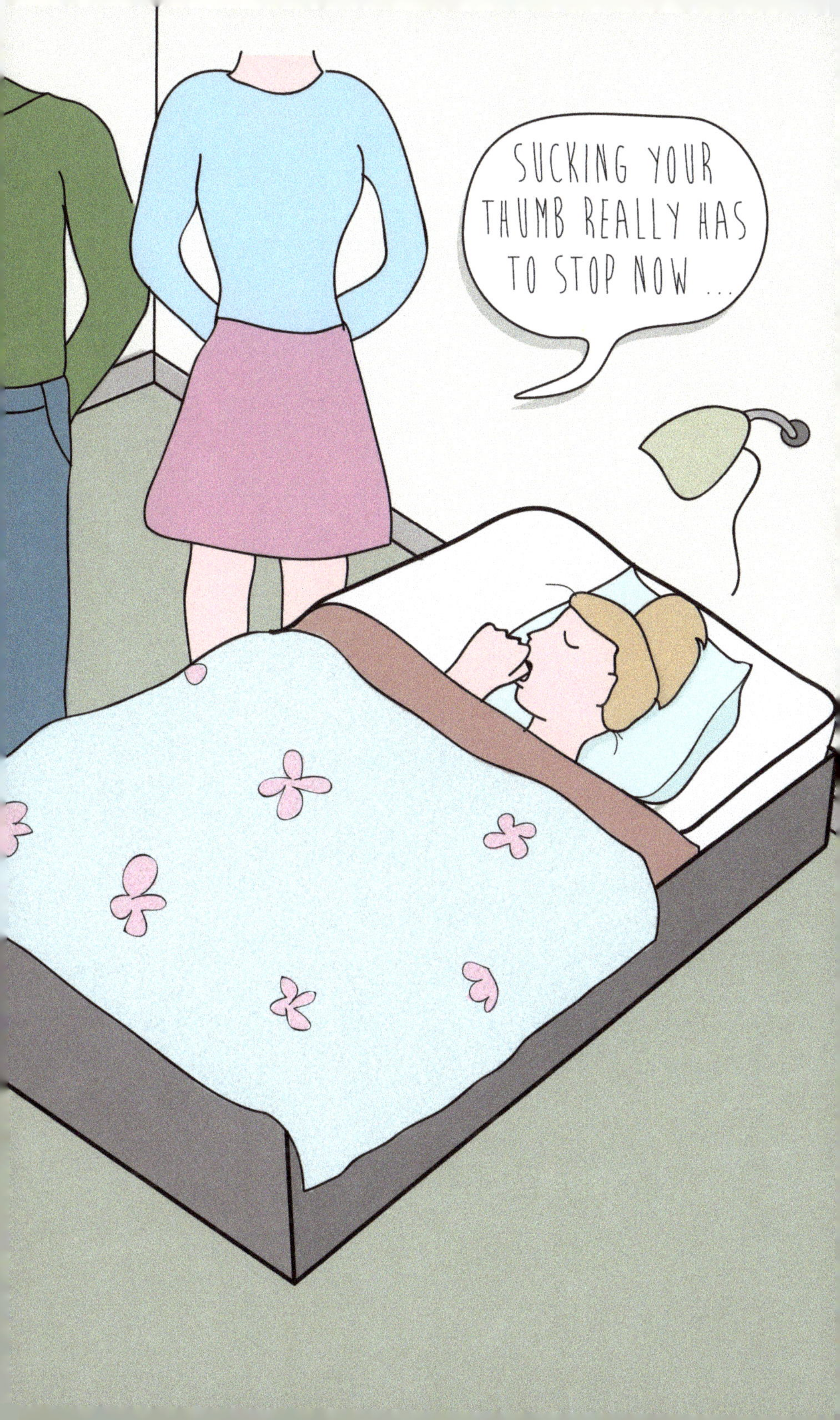
SUCKING YOUR THUMB REALLY HAS TO STOP NOW ...

The next day at breakfast mum says "I have to tell you something darling girl. It is time to stop the thumb sucking."

"Yes", says dad, "just give it a whirl."

"All that thumb sucking
makes that your teeth
come apart.
You are a big girl now,
already five.
Let your thumb free,
that really needs
to start."

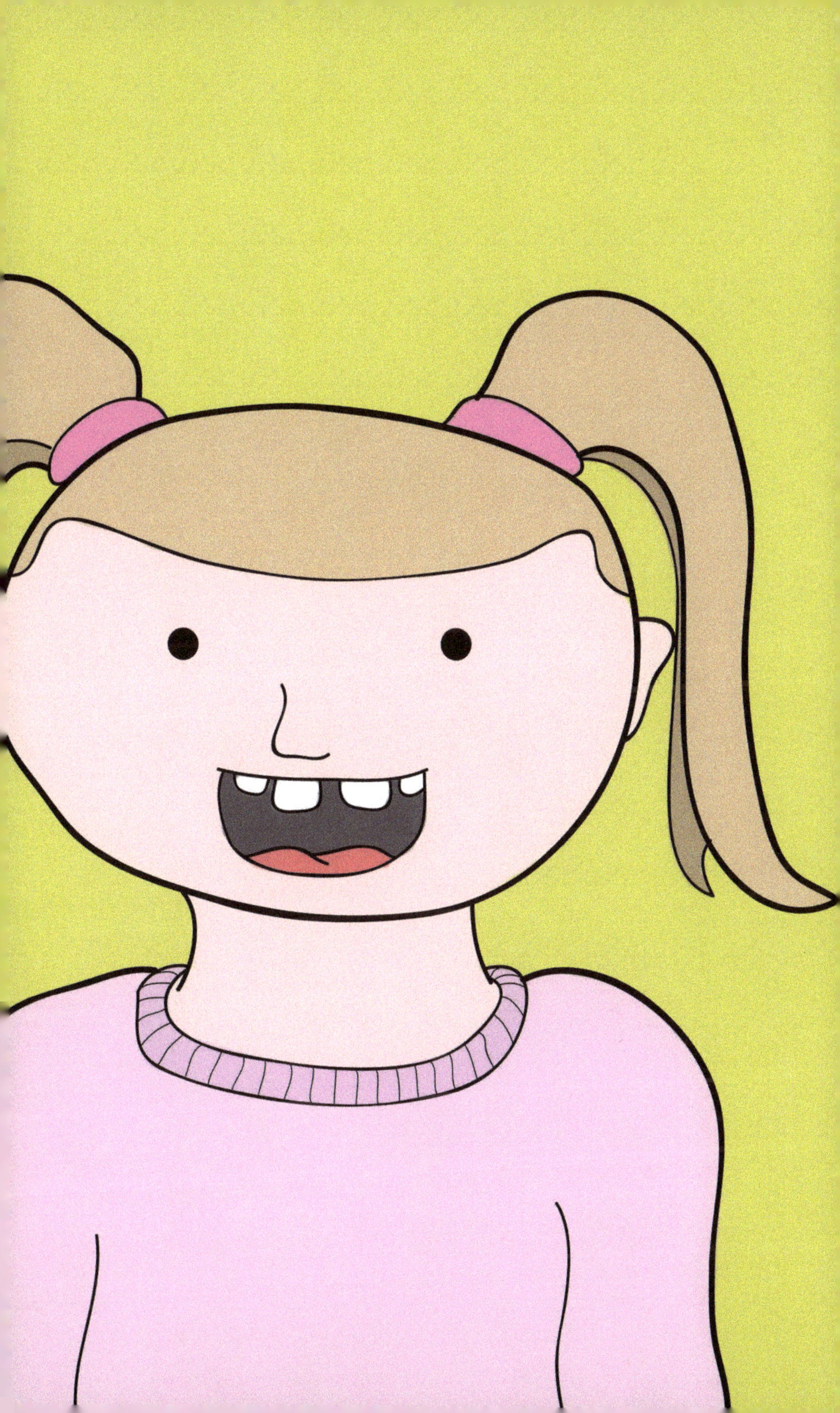

Giving up is difficult for Hetty
she can't do it on her own.
So mum rubs something on her thumb.
"It tastes wrong," says Hetty with a groan.

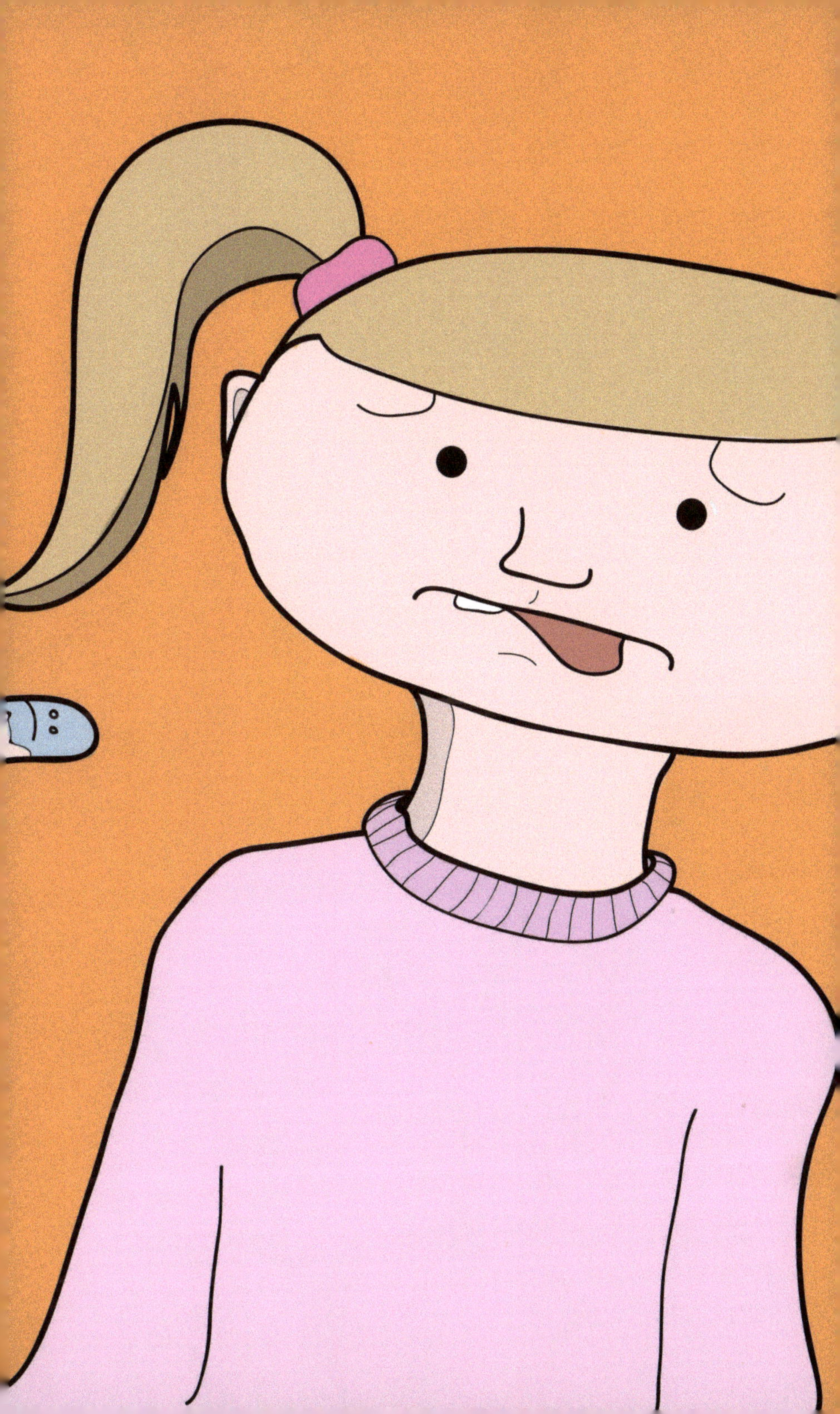

Sucking her thumb
has now an awful taste,
so Hetty doesn't bother.
Her teeth are really
happy with that
and stand more
next to each other.

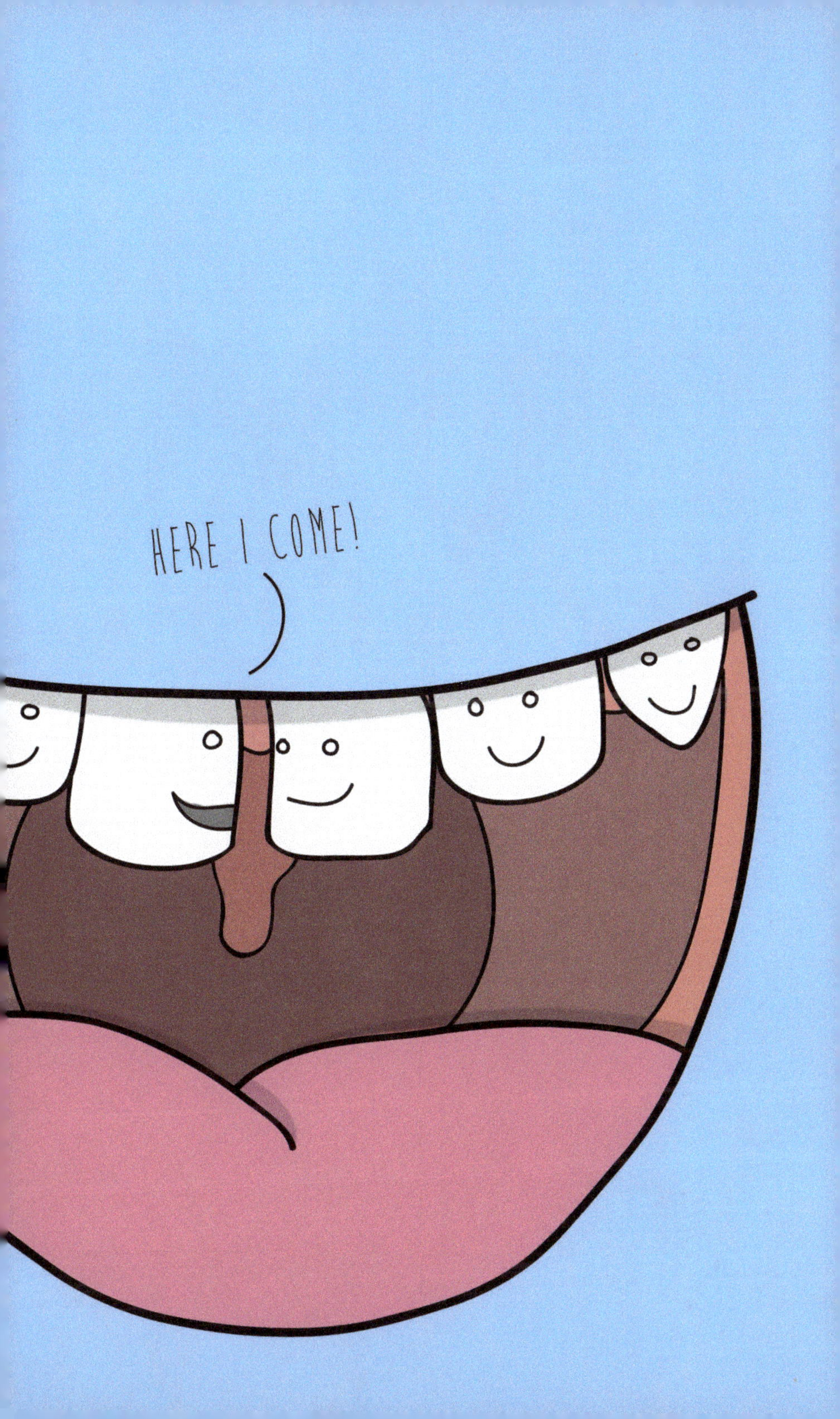
HERE I COME!

> EY, TONGUE! THERE YOU ARE!

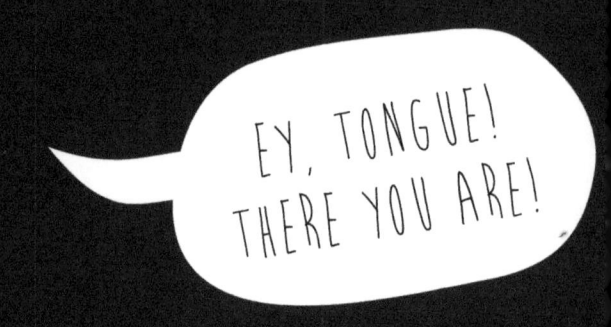

The tongue has
now more space
and is back in the top.
No more being pushed
by the thumb,
that finally did stop.

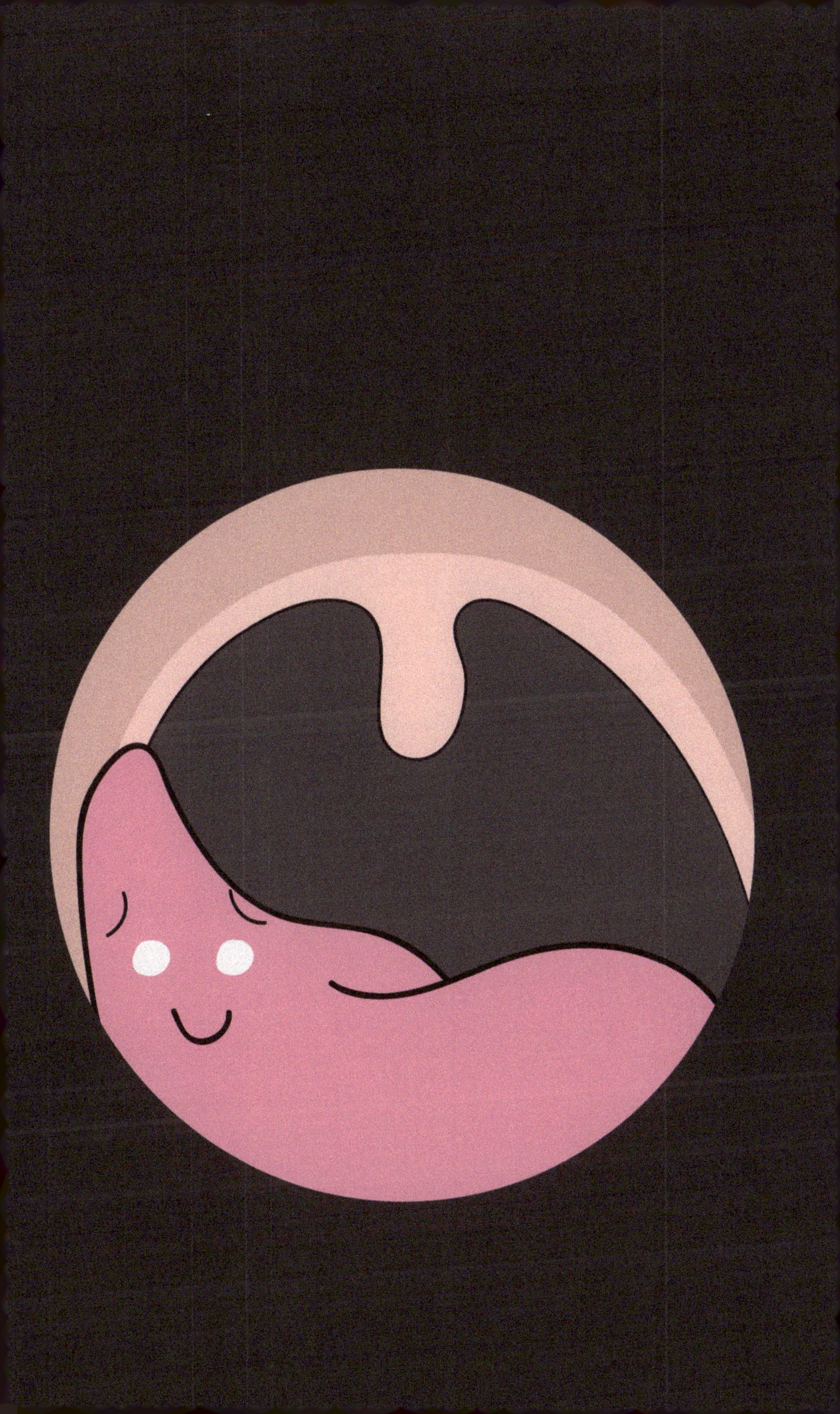

Hetty has her mouth closed now.
That's how it's supposed to be.
It is much more healthy and her thumb is happy and free!

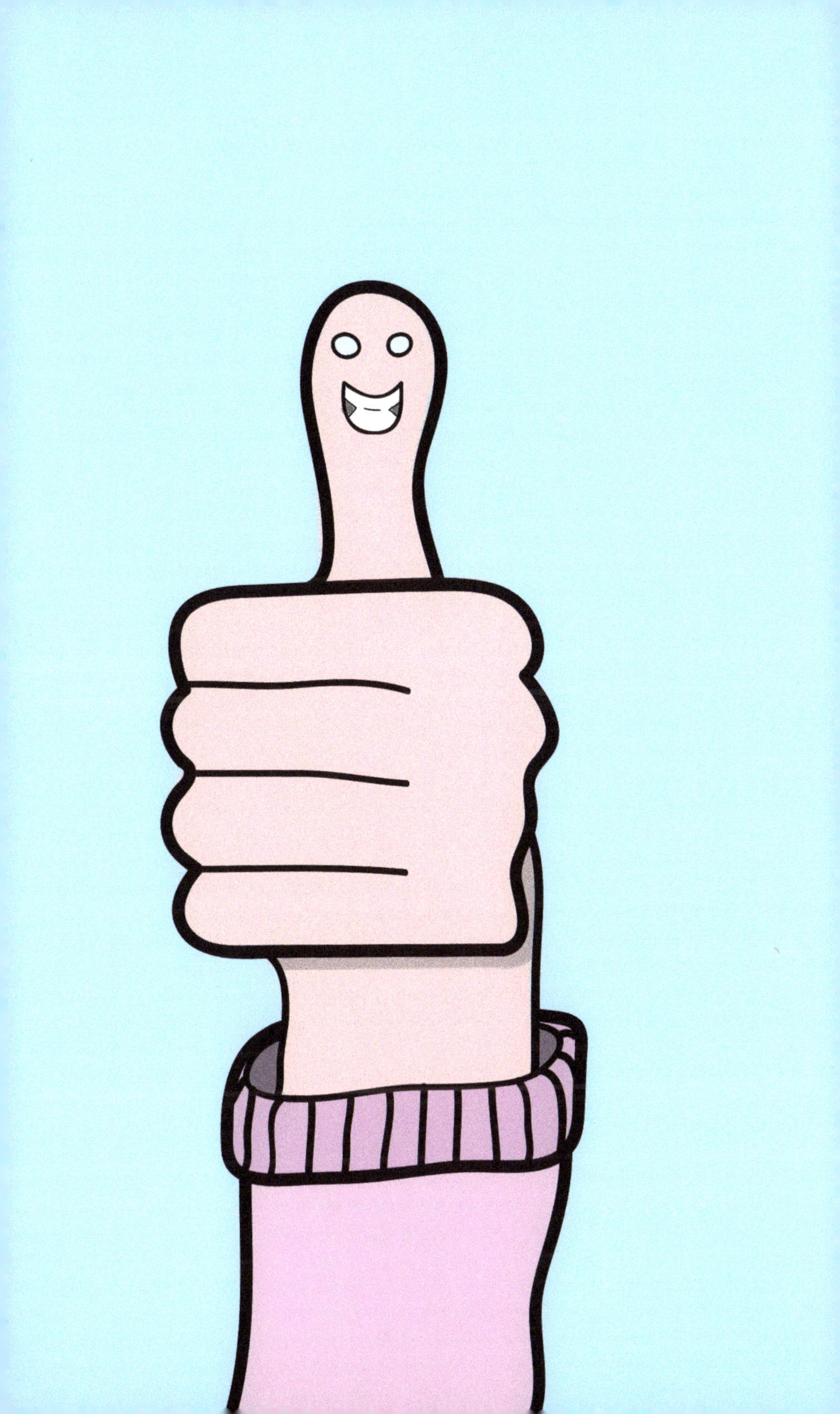